100 THINGS TO DO IN INDIANAPOLIS BEFORE YOU DIE

3rd Edition

Monument Circle
Courtesy of Kelly Harris, Indiana Landmarks

3rd Edition

100 THINGS TO DO IN INDIANAPOLIS BEFORE YOU DIE

ASHLEY PETRY

REEDY PRESS

Reedy Press
PO Box 5131
St. Louis, MO 63139, USA
reedypress.com

Library of Congress Control Number: 2025936459

ISBN: 9781681065922

Design by Jill Halpin

Cover photo courtesy of iStock

Unless otherwise noted, all photos are courtesy of the author or are believed to be in the public domain.

Printed in the United States of America
25 26 27 28 29 5 4 3 2 1

CONTENTS

Culture and History

Shopping and Fashion

INTRODUCTION

The first edition of this book was published exactly 10 years ago. Although I'd been writing about Indianapolis as a freelance journalist for years, it was my first book, and I was giddy. Since then I've published a few more books about Indianapolis, but this one still feels special—not only because it launched my publishing career but also because it gives me the opportunity to celebrate the very best of my hometown.

This freshly updated book is a bucket list of essential Circle City experiences. A certain auto race makes an appearance here, of course, as does the largest children's museum in the world. The book also covers the city's best restaurants, cultural attractions, music venues, historical sites, and recreational opportunities.

For visitors to Indianapolis, this book will help you pack your days with exciting and memorable food and fun. For locals, this book serves as a reminder to get out into the city and actually do those things you've been meaning to do for years now. And it also contains some activities that might surprise you.

When you complete these 100 things, your next step is the lesser-known activities in my *Secret Indianapolis: A Guide to the Weird, Wonderful, and Obscure.* For more background on the history of the city, check out *Indianapolis: An Illustrated Timeline* for a comprehensive overview and *Amazing Indianapolis* for a roundup of historical fun facts. All of those books exist because this book existed first, and for that I will be forever grateful.

Summer Nights Film Series
Courtesy of Newfields

ACKNOWLEDGMENTS

Every acknowledgments section I have written starts by thanking the incredible publishing team at Reedy Press, and there's a good reason for that. We have worked together for a decade now, and I am so proud of what we have created together. I deeply appreciate you.

I also want to thank the people throughout the city who have contributed to this book. You have answered my questions, shared your insider tips, contributed beautiful photos, and provided all sorts of guidance along the way. This includes business owners, communications professionals, fellow journalists, and tourism specialists, including the wonderful team at Visit Indy.

Finally, as always, I am grateful to my friends and family—you are so precious to me. To Brooke and Henry as always, forever. And to Michael, who cheerfully accompanied me on research missions all across the city. Thank you for your invaluable support.

The Garage Food Hall at Bottleworks
Courtesy of the Garage Food Hall

FOOD AND DRINK

1

SATISFY EVERY STOMACH
AT THE GARAGE FOOD HALL

Food halls are an international trend, and one beautifully executed example is the Garage, part of the downtown Bottleworks development. More than 20 vendors call the food hall home, serving up Asian-fusion tacos, Venezuelan arepas, British fish and chips, Cuban sandwiches, fresh smoothies, and Indian favorites. Other options include ramen, pizza, barbecue, sushi, and poké bowls. Local favorite Lick Ice Cream has a shop here, as does Indiana-based Hard Truth Distilling Co. With the Garage, there's no more arguing about which restaurant to try—everyone in your group can have exactly what they're craving.

906 Carrollton Ave., 317-556-1252
garageindy.com

TIP

The Garage Food Hall is also home to Pumkinfish, a fun gift shop that highlights artisan products made here in Indiana.

906 Carrollton Ave., 317-974-9167
pumkinfish.com

2

SNEAK INTO A SPEAKEASY

Plenty of Indianapolis cocktail bars have a speakeasy vibe. On Mass Ave alone you'll find the Ball & Biscuit, the basement Nowhere Special cocktail lounge, and the Wiseguy Lounge at Goodfellas Pizzeria. But only a few local hot spots are genuinely hard to find—or to get into once you find them. The Vault Indy on East Street requires a four-digit passcode. (Hint: It's a year.) The Commodore, located in the Fountain Square Theatre building, is behind a nondescript door near the lobby, although no password is required. But Bootleggers, located at the Flatiron on Penn, is the complete package—it's hard to find, *and* a password is required. Look behind the bar for an important clue. If you're stumped, ask the friendly staff for guidance. And if you make it inside, don't miss the pickle moonshine.

Bootleggers
605 N Pennsylvania St.

The Commodore
1107 Prospect St.

The Vault
1542 S East St.

3

TRY THAI-INSPIRED COCKTAILS
AT BODHI

Everything on the menu at BODHI looks familiar; dishes such as spring rolls, chicken curry, and pad Thai are available all across town. But this inventive restaurant in the former Black Market location will surprise you with its original and delicious takes on Thai classics. Named one of *USA Today*'s restaurants of the year in 2025, the bistro also has a clever cocktail menu highlighting Thai flavors such as ginger, tamarind, and lychee. Owned by three generations of a family of Thai women, it is rightfully one of the most popular restaurants in town. But it doesn't accept reservations, so expect waits of two hours or more at peak times.

922 Massachusetts Ave., 317-941-6595
bodhi-indy.com

4

VISIT THE WALK-UP WINDOW
AT MY SUGAR PIE

At My Sugar Pie, just off Main Street in Zionsville, you don't even have to go inside to order your Mom's Original Dutch Apple pie. The cute white cottage now has a walk-up window. Ask for a single slice to enjoy at a pink table on the patio, or pick up an entire pie to take home for later. At $40 and up, these pies aren't cheap, but they are definitely worth it—and you get to keep the glass pie dish. The Mom's Original made with sliced Granny Smith apples is a bestseller, along with Hoosier Sugar Cream. There's also a rotating menu of seasonal flavors.

40 E Pine St., 317-733-8717
mysugarpie.com

TIP

If you're closer to SoBro, consider the excellent Pots & Pans Pie Co., best known for its apple crumble and sugar crème brûlée pies. The shop also stocks savory take-and-bake pot pies. Savory pie + sweet pie = dinner + dessert = done.

4915 N College Ave., 317-600-3475, potsandpansindy.com

5

GET JAZZY
AT GERALDINE'S SUPPER CLUB

Picture the smoky haze of a dimly lit 1950s jazz club. That's what you'll find at Geraldine's Supper Club & Lounge, minus the smoke. The restaurant is off the beaten path, near Fletcher Place and Fountain Square in a nondescript building, so hearing the live music as you step inside feels like discovering a secret. The menu features classics like French onion soup, oysters Rockefeller, caviar, porterhouse steaks, rack of lamb, and surf and turf. It's not the friendliest menu for herbivores, but the daily risotto can be made vegetarian or vegan. There's also a menu of vintage cocktails and a long wine list. Reservations are recommended.

1101 English Ave., 317-600-3336
geraldinesindy.com

BET ON A CREATIVE BRUNCH AT MILKTOOTH

As the former chef de cuisine at the gone-but-not-forgotten Recess, Jonathan Brooks has some serious culinary street cred. So Indy locals have embraced his "fine diner," Milktooth, a hipster-friendly restaurant that serves "unconventionally creative morning fare" in a renovated garage. When it opened in 2015, it made *Food & Wine*'s list of the best new restaurants in America, and *Condé Nast Traveler* named it one of the 207 best restaurants in the *world*. The eatery offers clever twists on classic dishes, such as Dutch baby pancakes and ancient-grains porridge, "of the moment" specials, and side dishes such as sorghum-glazed bacon and pecan sticky buns. Few chefs, in Indy or anywhere, bring such a gourmet sensibility to the humble first meal of the day.

534 Virginia Ave., 317-986-5131
milktoothindy.com

7

HAVE A CULINARY ADVENTURE AT BLUEBEARD

Named after a novel by Kurt Vonnegut, Bluebeard mirrors the hometown author's creativity and irreverence. The James Beard Award semifinalist is a farm-to-table favorite and without doubt one of the best restaurants in Indianapolis. The ever-changing menu includes seasonal salads, house-made pastas and other entrées, and a variety of snacks and sides. (Don't miss the fried brussels sprouts.) There's also an excellent cocktail menu. Just be aware that your food might surprise you—I once ordered a pavlova that came as chunks of pastel meringue reminiscent of Fruity Pebbles. Yet it was delicious, like just about everything at this memorable restaurant.

653 Virginia Ave., 317-686-1580
bluebeardindy.com

8

DINE
AT THE DEHAAN ESTATE

Hidden from view on 150 wooded acres, the $14.5 million home of millionaire Christel DeHaan has long been a source of speculation and curiosity. But since her death, RH (formerly Restoration Hardware) has transformed the Palladian-style mansion—called Linden House—into a furniture showroom that is open to the public. You can explore the 41,000-square-foot house and its grounds, including a 35-acre private lake. Then book a table in the RH Dining Room at the heart of the house. The pricey menu reflects its surroundings: Lunch and dinner options include luxuries like caviar and lobster, along with salads, sandwiches, and steaks. Afterward, you might just find the perfect sofa.

4501 N Michigan Rd., 317-706-9670
rh.com/us/en/indianapolis

9

ENCOUNTER THE RED VELVET ELVIS
AT THE FLYING CUPCAKE BAKERY

The Flying Cupcake was Indy's first cupcake bakery, and it's still going strong. The shabby-chic bakery's display cases overflow with both regular and filled cupcakes, but you should start with the enormous Red Velvet Elvis. It's made with moist red velvet cake and chocolate chunks, and it's topped with rich cream cheese icing and shavings of white chocolate. Other favorites include the strawberry Pretty in Pink, the decadent chocolate ganache, and the salted caramel. The bakery also caters to dietary restrictions, offering vegan and gluten-free options at every location.

Downtown
423 N Massachusetts Ave.

Castleton
4026 E 82nd St.

Carmel
831 S Rangeline Rd., Ste. 300

317-396-2696
theflyingcupcakebakery.com

10

FIND THE SWEET SPOT
AT THE CAKE BAKE SHOP

A fairyland experience awaits inside the Cake Bake Shop's two locations. Festoons of flowers are interwoven with twinkling lights, crystal chandeliers drip from the ceilings, and edible glitter covers the cocktails and desserts. But the magical decor never overshadows the cakes, which tempt from beneath domes of glass. The three-layer Gwendolyn's Famous Earl's Court Chocolate Cake (named for owner Gwendolyn Rogers) has appeared on Food Network's *Guilty Pleasures*, and the mint-chocolate-chip cake has been featured in *O, The Oprah Magazine*. Stop by for a simple mimosa and macaron, or check out the Cake Bake Shop's French-inspired menu, which features salads, sandwiches, and the largest slices of quiche you've ever seen. The truly special afternoon tea service (reservations required) includes a tiered tray of finger sandwiches, pastries, and fresh-baked scones.

6515 Carrollton Ave.
800 S Rangeline Rd., Ste. 260, Carmel
317-257-2253
thecakebakeshop.com

TIP

Look closely at the servers' name tags, which reveal their favorite cake flavors.

11

SEARCH FOR INDY'S
BEST SOUL FOOD

If you're on a quest for comfort food, look no further than the homestyle cooking at Indy's best soul food restaurants. One local favorite is Kountry Kitchen Soul Food Place, which serves plates heaped high with meatloaf, smothered pork chops, and crispy fried chicken, all served with fresh-baked cornbread and pitchers of sweet tea. With two locations, His Place Eatery offers chicken and waffles, barbecue ribs, and made-from-scratch chicken and dumplings; *Indianapolis Monthly* calls it "some of the most flavorful food in town." And for sheer bounty, you can't beat Mississippi Belle, a family-style restaurant where platters of fried chicken, slow-roasted pork, meatloaf, and fried fish are refilled until you can't eat one more bite.

His Place Eatery
6916 E 30th St., 317-545-4890
1411 W 86th St., 317-790-3406
hisplaceeatery.com

Kountry Kitchen
1831 N College Ave., 317-635-6000
kountrykitchenindy.com

Mississippi Belle
2170 E 54th St., 317-466-0522
mississippibelleindy.com

12

DEVOUR THE CITY'S BEST SANDWICH

AT GOOSE THE MARKET

When Chris Eley opened Smoking Goose in 2007, he brought craft butchery back to Indianapolis. Now his charcuterie appears on the menus of every farm-to-fork restaurant in the city. But for the best Goose has to offer, you must go straight to the source: Goose the Market. *Bon Appétit* named it one of the 10 best sandwich shops in the nation, so head to the deli counter and order a Batali, a sandwich made with spicy coppa; salt-cured capocollo; and soppressata, a dry Italian salami. Toppings include tomato preserves, provolone cheese, hot giardiniera, marinated red onions, mayo, and romaine. Take your sandwich downstairs to the cozy basement *enoteca*, where foodies gather at the communal tables, surrounded by racks of craft beers and superb wines.

2503 N Delaware St., 317-924-4944
goosethemarket.com

TIP

Fans of artisan charcuterie should sign up for a behind-the-scenes tour at the Smoking Goose smokehouse on Saturday mornings. You'll learn about different smoking techniques, see the variety of products in the aging room, and finish with a guided tasting.

407 Dorman St., 317-638-6328
smokinggoose.com

TRY THE TENDERLOIN
AT BONGE'S TAVERN

It's worth the trek to Perkinsville for Indiana's signature dish, the breaded pork tenderloin. Founded in 1934, Bonge's Tavern—where regulars tailgate in the parking lot before their reservations—cooks up a juicy parmesan-crusted version topped with lemon butter, served with mashed potatoes and jalapeño corn bread. The menu also includes duck breast, steaks, lamb chops, fish, and a house-made pasta of the day (which can be made vegetarian). Enormous slabs of prime rib are available on weekends. Reservations are essential for this small space, which is decorated with Christmas lights, vintage sports pennants, and plastic tablecloths—a simple setting for such delicious food. Save room for the signature sugar cream cake, served with warm blueberries and fresh whipped cream.

9830 W 280 N, Perkinsville, 765-734-1625
bongestavern.com

14

ORDER THE CINNAMON TOAST
AT CAFE PATACHOU

Founded in 1989, Cafe Patachou was the first foray for local restaurateur Martha Hoover, who now operates restaurants all over the city. The "student union for adults" specializes in elevated breakfast and brunch fare, especially omelets and broken-yolk sandwiches. *Bon Appétit* once named it one of the nation's top 10 breakfast spots, and I'm guessing it was because of the cinnamon toast. Thick slabs of warm sourdough bread are sliced to order, buttered, and generously topped with cinnamon and sugar. Cafe Patachou now has eight locations in Indianapolis and the northside suburbs of Carmel, Fishers, and Zionsville, but the original is at 49th and Pennsylvania Streets.

cafepatachou.com

TIP

Martha Hoover's other restaurant concepts include the French champagne bistro Petite Chou and the artisanal Napolese pizzeria.

15

PICK THE PERFECT PUMPKIN
AT TUTTLE ORCHARDS

Located just east of Indianapolis, Tuttle Orchards is a fourth-generation family farm founded in 1928. It has a year-round farm store and café, fresh produce in season, and gardening workshops for beginners. But the busiest season is fall, when the orchard offers apple picking, a pumpkin patch, and a flower garden where you can cut your own bouquet. The fall farm experience also includes wagon rides, a corn maze, outdoor family games, goat and llama meet and greets, and lots of play areas for children. Insider tip: Buy a frozen apple pie to bake later at home. Note that the farm is closed on Sundays.

5717 N 300 W, Greenfield, 317-326-2278
indianapolisorchard.com

OTHER YOU-PICK OPTIONS

Driving Wind Farm

6410 Michigan Rd., 317-492-9512
drivingwindberryfarm.com

Spencer Farm

7177 E 161st St., Noblesville, 317-776-1560
spencerberryfarm.com

Stuckey Farm

19975 Hamilton Boone Rd., Sheridan
317-769-4636
stuckeyfarm.com

Waterman's Family Farm

7010 E Raymond St., 317-356-6995
watermansfamilyfarm.com

16

EXPERIENCE INDY'S
OLD-SCHOOL HANGOUTS

Indianapolis offers plenty of options for vintage ambiance, whether you're envisioning a drive-in restaurant or a sit-down café. For drive-in nostalgia, head to Mug-n-Bun, which was founded in 1960. It is best known for its burgers, hand-dipped onion rings, and house-made root beer. Indy's Historic Steer-In Restaurant was founded as a drive-in, also in 1960; it no longer offers curb service, but in the dining room you can order from a diner menu that includes all-day breakfast and pork tenderloin sandwiches. Finally, grab a booth at the Rock-Cola 50's Cafe. Although it was founded in the 1990s, it oozes vintage Americana. This is the only place in the world where you can still order Choc-Ola, a chocolate drink similar to Yoo-hoo that was developed in Indianapolis in the 1940s and bottled here for decades.

Indy's Historic Steer-In Restaurant
5130 E 10th St., Speedway, 317-356-0996
steerin.net

Mug-n-Bun Drive-In
5211 W 10th St., Speedway, 317-244-5669
mug-n-bun.com

Rock-Cola 50's Cafe
5730 S Brookville Rd., 317-357-2233
rock-cola-50s-cafe.foodjoyy.com

17

GET SMASHED BURGERS
AT WORKINGMAN'S FRIEND

Before Indy had mixology bars and artisan pizzerias, it had dives like Workingman's Friend. The historic restaurant was founded in 1918 by a Macedonian immigrant, Louis Stamatkin, who originally called the place Belmont Lunch. The restaurant earned its current name in 1922, when it began accepting IOUs from local railroad workers who had gone on strike. Today the no-frills, cash-only diner is best known for its $5 smashed burgers—thin beef patties with crispy edges. Order a cheeseburger and a side of onion rings for the true Workingman's Friend experience. It is frequently voted the best cheeseburger in town. But as you would expect in Indiana, pork tenderloin is on the menu here, as well.

234 N Belmont Ave., 317-636-2067

SHOP LOCAL
AT THE BROAD RIPPLE FARMERS MARKET

Indianapolis has plenty of neighborhood farmers markets, but nobody does it better than Broad Ripple. Founded in 1994, the year-round Broad Ripple Farmers Market is now the largest in the state. About 85 vendors participate in the summer months, and about 60 stay on through the winter. Check out flavored olive oils from Artisano's Oil & Spices, craft hard cider from Ash & Elm, or preserves and pickled veggies from Home Ec Preserves. You'll also find seasonal produce, frozen meats, fresh breads and pastries, flowers and potted plants, local honey, hot sauces, and artisan cheeses, plus ready-to-eat foods like hummus and soup. The market is open on Saturday mornings, rain or shine, so you can start planning your meals for the following week—or simply pick up a foodie souvenir of your time in Indianapolis.

Summer location:
Glendale Town Center, 6001 N Rural St.

Winter location:
Broad Ripple Middle School, 1115 Broad Ripple Ave.

317-251-2782
broadrippleindy.org/farmers-market

19

SIP A TASTY CIDER

AT ASH & ELM

Indianapolis still mourns New Day Meadery and its hard ciders, but Ash & Elm Cider Co. has filled the gap beautifully. Its "complex, drinkable, apple-forward" hard ciders are made with fresh-pressed Indiana apple juice, all-natural fruit infusions, and whole spices. The company, with tasting rooms in both downtown Indianapolis and Carmel, was founded by Aaron and Andréa Homoya in 2016 after they sampled ciders on a trip to Ireland. Start with the bestselling Fleeting Youth, a tart blend with raspberries and lemons. Other flagship flavors include the Landstone Dry, Wayfinder Semi Sweet, and award-winning Sunset Tart Cherry.

1301 E Washington St., 317-600-3164
525 North End Dr., Ste. 190, Carmel, 317-740-1991
ashandelmcider.com

TIP

Join the Ash & Elm Cider Club to receive monthly or quarterly shipments of seasonal and limited-edition flavors.

20

VISIT A HOMEGROWN DISTILLERY
AT HOTEL TANGO

When the weather outside is frightful, curl up with a rum-spiked apple cider near the crackling fireplace in Hotel Tango Distillery's rustic Fletcher Place tasting room. The artisan distillery (not actually a hotel) was founded by Marine veteran Travis Barnes and his wife, Hilary, and its name consists of the owners' initials in the military phonetic alphabet. The distillery's spirits include the usual offerings—bourbon, rye whiskey, and vodka—as well as flavored bourbons in pumpkin spice, toasted marshmallow, and hot chocolate. According to the labels, they're all "distilled with discipline." While you're here, order a tasting flight or one of the stellar craft cocktails and sneak a peek at the on-site stills.

702 Virginia Ave., 317-653-1806
hoteltangodistillery.com

MORE LOCAL DISTILLERIES

8th Day Distillery

1125 E Brookside Ave., 317-600-3791
8thdaydistillery.com

Four Finger Distillery

630 Virginia Ave., 317-974-9862
fourfingerdistillery.com

Moon Drops Distillery

738 W Broadway St., Fortville, 317-482-9392
moondropsdistillery.com

West Fork Whiskey Co.

10 E 191st St., Westfield, 317-763-5400
westforkwhiskey.com

21

WORSHIP THE SUN GOD
AT SUN KING BREWERY

The biggest name in Indy brewing is Sun King. In 2015, its rapid growth forced Indiana legislators to increase the legal cap on the number of barrels a microbrewery could produce each year. Its best-selling beers—the Osiris Pale Ale, Wee Mac Scottish-style Ale, Pachanga Mexican-style Lager, Sunlight Cream Ale, and others—are available just about everywhere in Central Indiana, even in bars that sell mostly Bud Light. At the three Indy-area tasting rooms, you can order a beer or tasting flight, or refill your Sun King growler. To learn more about the brewing process, sign up for a facility tour downtown and hear the incredible story of this local favorite's success.

Downtown
135 N College Ave., 317-602-3702

Fishers
9713 District N Dr., 317-436-1926

Carmel
351 Monon Blvd., 317-843-6250

sunkingbrewing.com

MORE LOCAL BREWERIES

Bier Brewery & Taproom
5133 E 65th St.
317-253-2437
bierbrewery.com

Broad Ripple Brewpub
842 E 65th St.
317-253-2739
broadripplemenu.com

Centerpoint Brewing Company
1125 E Brookside Ave.
317-602-8386
centerpointbrewing.com

Chilly Water Brewing Company
719 Virginia Ave.
317-964-0518
chillywaterbrewing.com

Deviate Brewing
4004 W 96th St.
317-374-8429
deviatebrewing.com

Fountain Square Brew Co.
1301 Barth Ave.
463-274-3763
fountainsquare.beer

Four Day Ray Brewing
11671 Lantern Rd., Fishers, 317-343-0200
fourdayray.com

Guggman Haus Brewing Co.
1701 Gent Ave.
317-602-6131
guggmanhausbrewing.com

MashCraft Brewing
Three Indianapolis locations
mashcraft.com

Metazoa Brewing Co.
140 S College Ave.
317-522-0251
metazoabrewing.com

St. Joseph Brewery
540 N College Ave.
317-602-5670
saintjoseph.beer

Taxman Brewing Co.
310 S Delaware St.
317-734-3107
taxmanbrewing.com

Upland Brewing Co.
Five Indianapolis locations uplandbeer.com

22

TASTE THE TRAMINETTE
AT A LOCAL WINERY

A Midwestern hybrid, the Traminette grape is well-suited for Hoosier weather. First planted in Indiana in the early 1990s, it has since become the state's signature wine grape. Start your tasting journey at Buck Creek Winery, the only commercial vineyard in Indianapolis, where wine slushies are a popular treat. The award-winning Easley Winery has a tasting room downtown, while Daniel's Family Vineyard & Winery offers "a genuine wine country experience" on its 22 acres in McCordsville. Brandywine Creek Vineyards & Winery is just southeast of Indianapolis, while Mallow Run Winery is due south on a family farm in Bargersville. Its motto: "Work hard. Picnic often." Check the winery calendars for upcoming events such as yoga classes, crafting workshops, live music, trivia nights, and vineyard tours.

LOCAL WINERIES

Brandywine Creek Vineyards & Winery

12524 Southeastern Ave., 317-868-0563
brandywinecreekvineyards.com

Buck Creek Winery

11747 Indian Creek Rd. S, 317-862-9463
buckcreekwinery.com

Daniel's Family Vineyard & Winery

9061 N 700 W, McCordsville, 317-248-5222
danielsvineyard.com

Easley Winery

205 N College Ave., 317-636-4516
easleywinery.com

Mallow Run Winery

6964 W Whiteland Rd., Bargersville, 317-422-1556
mallowrun.com

FIND YOUR FAVORITE
FINE DINING

Not so long ago, fine dining in Indianapolis meant chain steak houses and . . . other chain steak houses. Not anymore. The city's restaurant renaissance has made it easy to choose a unique dining experience for special occasions.

For romantic ambiance, your best bets are Meridian Restaurant & Bar, Mama Carolla's, Ocean Prime, and Tinker Street. Late Harvest Kitchen and Oakleys Bistro are chef-driven northside restaurants with ever-changing seasonal menus. Meanwhile, the Fountain Room is a great option in the Bottleworks district. A few other favorites have their own entries in this book: Bluebeard, St. Elmo Steak House, the Loft at Traders Point Creamery, and the Cunningham group.

TIP

For a drink before or after dinner, try the rooftop bar at the InterContinental. Astrea offers lovely views of both the Statehouse and Monument Circle, especially after dark.

17 W Market St., 11th floor, 463-303-0400
astrearooftop.com

TOP OPTIONS FOR FINE DINING

The Fountain Room

830 Massachusetts Ave., 463-238-4464
thefountainroom.com

Late Harvest Kitchen

8605 River Crossing Blvd., 317-663-8063
lateharvestkitchen.com

Mama Carolla's

1031 E 54th St., 317-259-9412
mamacarollas.com

Meridian Restaurant & Bar

5694 N Meridian St., 317-466-1111
meridianonmeridian.com

Oakleys Bistro

1464 W 86th St., 317-824-1231
oakleysbistro.com

Ocean Prime

8555 N River Rd., 317-569-0975
oceanprimeindy.com

Tinker Street

402 E 16th St., 317-925-5000
tinkerstreetrestaurant.com

EAT MORE, SPEND LESS

Can't afford to splurge on fine dining? Skip the national fast-food chains and try a local option for cheap eats. Start at Yats, which serves Cajun and Creole specialties like jambalaya and chili cheese étouffée. Entrées cost $10, including rice and garlic bread, and the menu changes daily. For inexpensive pho and other Vietnamese favorites, check out Egg Roll #1 on South Emerson Avenue. And for cheap eats with a Mexican flair, try the Tamale Place, where tamales cost from $3.75 to $5.45. The menu includes spicy options, such as chipotle chicken; mild options, such as pork in green sauce; several vegetarian options; and dessert tamales. You can also pick up a bag of frozen tamales for later.

Egg Roll #1
4540 S Emerson Ave., 317-787-2225
eggroll1.com

The Tamale Place
5226 Rockville Rd., 317-248-9771
thetamaleplace.com

Yats
Nine Central Indiana locations
yatscajuncreole.com

REAP THE CUNNINGHAM REWARDS

Many of Indy's most innovative restaurants have one thing in common: they're operated by the local Cunningham Restaurant Group, which has fueled the city's culinary renaissance. So it makes sense to sign up for the Cunningham VIP card: You'll earn a point for every dollar you spend, and a thousand points get you a $100 gift card.

To earn those points, head to the epicenter of Cunningham's creativity: Mass Ave. Bru Burger Bar has fabulous burgers, and Modita (located at the Bottleworks Hotel) serves Asian-inspired cuisine. Union 50 has a seasonal menu and live music, while Mesh offers fine dining in a more intimate setting. Vida, known for its eye-catching hydroponic wall of greens, is easily a contender for the city's best restaurant. But my personal favorite is Livery, which serves Latin-inspired dishes; think empanadas, yuca fries, pork belly tacos, and churros. Other Cunningham restaurants include Nesso, Shin Dig, Stone Creek Dining Company, Boulder Creek Dining Company, Cafe 251, Charbonos, Provision, Rize, Commission Row, and Tavern at the Point.

crgdining.com

26

EXPLORE INDY'S "LITTLE UNITED NATIONS" IN LAFAYETTE SQUARE

Once a case study in urban decay, the Lafayette Square neighborhood is now a hot spot for ethnic eats. Dubbed the "little United Nations" by the *New York Times*, its official designation is the International Marketplace. Chapati is known for Indian and Pakistani street foods, as well as outstanding halal fried chicken. Try Pho Saigon or King Wok for Vietnamese cuisine, Havana Café for Cuban favorites, and Machu Picchu for Peruvian specialties, such as *lomo saltado* and *chicha morada*. Abyssinia serves eat-with-your-fingers Ethiopian cuisine, including an elaborate coffee service. And despite being tucked inside a grocery store, Carniceria Guanajuato is the city's top spot for authentic Mexican food. Saraga, the city's best international grocery store, has a location in this neighborhood, too.

INTERNATIONAL DINING IN LAFAYETTE SQUARE

Abyssinia Ethiopian Restaurant
5352 W 38th St., 317-299-0608
abyssiniaindy.com

Carniceria Guanajuato
5210 W Pike Plaza Rd., 317-490-5060

Chapati
4930 Lafayette Rd., Ste. G, 317-405-9874
eatchapati.com

Havana Café
3839 Moller Rd., 317-293-2822

King Wok
4150 Lafayette Rd., 317-295-8090
kingwokindy.com

Machu Picchu
5356 W 38th St., 317-388-8696

Pho Saigon
4760 W 38th St., 317-927-7270
phosaigonindianapolis.com

Saraga International Grocery
3605 Commercial Dr., 317-388-9999
saragaindy.com

ENJOY A RURAL RETREAT
AT TRADERS POINT CREAMERY

Tucked away in the woods near Zionsville, Traders Point Creamery is a delightful surprise. Happy, grass-fed cows produce organic milk for ice cream, yogurt, cheese, and the best cottage cheese you'll ever eat. The farm is open for tours and operates a small store, but the real draw is the charming Loft Restaurant, which is housed in a converted barn. Beneath the exposed wooden beams of the ceiling, you'll dine on farm-to-fork favorites such as cheese and charcuterie platters, fresh-caught fish, and grass-fed steaks. Don't skip dessert from the Dairy Bar, which serves house-made ice cream in vanilla, chocolate, and seasonal flavors. When your rural retreat is over, you'll be amazed at how quickly you find yourself back in the bustle of the city.

9101 Moore Rd., Zionsville, 317-733-1700
traderspointcreamery.com

GIVE IN TO GLUTTONY
AT THE INDIANA STATE FAIR

Forget about counting calories: the Indiana State Fair is the place to splurge on once-a-year treats such as deep-fried Oreo cookies, sugary lemon shake-ups, and butter-soaked corn on the cob. I always start at the Dairy Bar, where Hoosier dairy farmers serve up grilled cheese sandwiches and milkshakes. The Indiana Beef Cattle Association offers ribeye sandwiches, and Indiana Pork serves barbecue pulled pork—plus Indiana's signature dish, pork tenderloin sandwiches. Be on the lookout for the latest deep-fried food; past examples have included butter and bubble gum. You can break up the feeding frenzy with the fair's many activities, such as livestock competitions, concerts, and a midway full of rides and carnival games. As Rodgers and Hammerstein wrote, "Our state fair is a great state fair. Don't miss it. Don't even be late."

1202 E 38th St., 317-927-7500
indianastatefair.com

BRING THE FAMILY TOGETHER
AT HOLLYHOCK HILL

Hollyhock Hill was founded in 1928, when V. D. Vincent and his wife transformed their country cottage into a dining destination. Not much about the menu has changed since then; the restaurant still serves traditional home cooking. It is best known for its fried chicken, and that's what you should order, at least on your first visit. Other entrée options include shrimp, filet mignon, and seared salmon. Regardless of the protein selection, all entrées come with family-style portions of salad, mashed potatoes, gravy, corn, green beans, and piping hot biscuits with apple butter. Ice cream is included for dessert. Make a reservation, especially if you're coming with a large group.

8110 N College Ave., 317-251-2294
hollyhockhill.com

ORDER A SIMPLE YET PERFECT DOUGHNUT
AT LONG'S BAKERY

You *could* go to a craft doughnut shop and spend $5 on a ring of dough with exotic toppings. But it wouldn't be as good as a glazed yeast doughnut from Long's Bakery, which has been serving Indy's sweet tooth since 1955. The simple doughnut is light, fluffy, and melt-in-your-mouth delicious—and here that same $5 will get you several yummy treats. Unlike other bakeries that prepare doughnuts in bulk early in the morning, Long's Bakery continues to serve fresh, warm batches all day long. You must come prepared to pay cash and wait in line, but you'll soon learn to overlook the inconveniences.

1453 N Tremont St., 317-632-3741
2301 E Southport Rd., 317-783-1442
longsbakery.com

RELISH A CLASSIC REUBEN
AT SHAPIRO'S DELICATESSEN

Founded as a humble grocery store in 1905, Shapiro's Delicatessen is now a regional destination, serving the same corned beef and pastrami as New York City's storied kosher delis. Order the famous Reuben sandwich, made with slow-cooked corned beef, tangy sauerkraut, Swiss cheese, and Thousand Island dressing, sandwiched between hand-cut slices of house-baked rye bread. Or try an old-fashioned favorite, such as smoked tongue, matzo ball soup, chopped liver, or cabbage borscht. The cafeteria-style restaurant also has a tempting selection of pies, cakes, and cheesecakes, plus breakfast items like bagels and lox.

808 S Meridian St., 317-631-4041
shapiros.com

FEEL THE BURN
AT ST. ELMO STEAK HOUSE

If you eat at just one restaurant in Indianapolis, it should probably be St. Elmo Steak House. In business since 1902, the renowned Illinois Street eatery is still the best place to spot celebrities such as race car drivers and Indianapolis Colts players. But the real draw is the legendary shrimp cocktail, which contains so much horseradish that it can literally take your breath away. The rest of the menu is primarily seafood and steaks, including pricey but delicious USDA Prime dry-aged beef. After your meal, take a stroll over to the Soldiers and Sailors Monument, which was dedicated the same year the restaurant opened for business.

127 S Illinois St., 317-635-0636
stelmos.com

The Palladium concert hall in Carmel
Courtesy of the Center for the Performing Arts

MUSIC AND ENTERTAINMENT

VISIT CARMEL'S
STUNNING CONCERT HALL

If the Palladium reminds you of a European opera house, you're not alone. The concert hall is beautiful inside and out, and the acoustics are absolute perfection. It's the centerpiece of the Center for the Performing Arts, which is in turn the centerpiece of Carmel's massive City Center development. Under the artistic direction of Grammy-nominated crooner Michael Feinstein, the Palladium draws performers such as Emmylou Harris, Peter Frampton, and Itzhak Perlman. The audience skews a bit older than other local music venues, but that doesn't mean you need to rent a tuxedo or commission a couture gown; the Palladium prides itself on its casual vibe. On the other hand, thanks to several car dealerships' sponsorship of the valet service, you do get free valet parking if you show up in a Jaguar or Land Rover.

1 Carter Green, Carmel, 317-843-3800
thecenterfortheperformingarts.com

CATCH A FLICK
AT KAN-KAN

The city's only independent, nonprofit movie theater specializes in offbeat offerings, including cult classics, artsy new releases, and films that highlight marginalized communities. There's an annual festival of cat videos, as well as a film series for families. Don't be late for your showing; staff members sometimes give brief talks beforehand to place movies in their historical and cultural context. The concession stand offers the usual popcorn and candy, but Kan-Kan also has a full restaurant and bar.

1258 Windsor St., 317-800-7099
kankanindy.com

TIP

The Kan-Kan restaurant periodically closes for a menu revamp, so check the website before you make your dinner plans.

35

PLAY FROGGER
AT A RETRO ARCADE BAR

At Indy's two adults-only arcade bars, you can play classic games like Frogger, Centipede, Pac-Man, Mario Bros., and Donkey Kong, plus dozens more. No quarters or tokens needed—if you buy a drink, you play for free. Located downtown, 16-Bit Bar + Arcade (part of a multicity chain) is the larger of the two spaces, with Skee-Ball lanes, a two-story slide, and a giant Lite-Brite wall. Locally owned Tappers Arcade Bar in Fountain Square packs a similar number of games into a smaller space with a more traditional arcade vibe. Tappers also has more than two dozen vintage pinball machines, but for those you'll need your quarters. Either bar makes for a nostalgic night out.

16-Bit Bar + Arcade
110 E New York St., 317-939-6916
16-bitbar.com/indy

Tappers Arcade Bar
501 Virginia Ave., 317-602-6411
tappersarcadebar.com

SAMPLE THE SUMMER NIGHTS FILM SERIES AT NEWFIELDS

On Friday evenings in summer, bring a blanket and your favorite picnic fare to the outdoor terrace at the Indianapolis Museum of Art at Newfields. As part of its Summer Nights film series, the museum screens classic films like *Vertigo* and *Breakfast at Tiffany's*, as well as nostalgic favorites like *Dirty Dancing* and *The Princess Bride*. Trust me, you haven't seen *Dirty Dancing* properly until you've seen it under the stars, glass of wine in hand, surrounded by a crowd of people who cheer when Baby finally pulls off that lift. Tickets often sell out, so be sure to book early.

4000 Michigan Rd., 317-923-1331
discovernewfields.org

37

GO DOWN THE RABBIT HOLE AT THE WHITE RABBIT CABARET

For sheer weirdness, it's hard to beat the performance lineup at the White Rabbit Cabaret. The Fountain Square venue presents some things you might expect: live music, dance parties, stand-up comedy, and improv. But it also hosts fake author talks, drag shows, and dubious film screenings—think 1988's *Big Top Pee-wee*. Don't miss the monthly Burlesque Bingo Bango Show or the oddball Let's Make a Date game show. White Rabbit is also the home of Rocket Doll Revue, Indy's premier burlesque troupe. Its shows are a body-positive delight—more irreverent than salacious—and are perfect for a raucous girls' night out.

1116 Prospect St., 317-686-9550
whiterabbitcabaret.com

38

GET SILVER SCREEN SAVINGS
AT THE TIBBS DRIVE-IN THEATRE

Founded in 1967, the Tibbs Drive-In Theatre offers nostalgic summer fun. It's also an incredible bargain. The city's only surviving drive-in theater has four screens, and each screen shows two movies per night—one at dusk and one closer to midnight. The $12 admission price includes both showings. You can save even more money by bringing your own food and drinks. Veteran Tibbs customers arrive early and tailgate, setting up folding chairs on the lawn or converting their SUV trunks into temporary sofas. Sound is transmitted via FM radio, with a different frequency for each screen.

480 S Tibbs Ave., 317-243-6666
tibbsdriveintheatre.com

COME TO THE CABARET

As Sally Bowles sings in *Cabaret*, "What good is sitting alone in your room? Come hear the music play." Located downtown, the swanky dinner-and-a-show Cabaret brings in top-notch Broadway singers, jazz performers, and international cabaret stars for "a full evening of refined revelry." Past performers have included Ana Gasteyer, Alan Cumming, Megan Mullally, *Glee* star Darren Criss, and Tituss Burgess of *Unbreakable Kimmy Schmidt*. Plan to arrive at least an hour early to order from the dinner menu, which was developed by the Jazz Kitchen. Entrée options include a red wine braised short rib, miso-glazed salmon, and vegetarian butternut squash ravioli.

924 N Pennsylvania St., 317-275-1169
thecabaret.org

TIP

One of the Cabaret's most popular performances is its annual "Big Broadway Sing-Along: Holiday Edition" in early December. Book tickets early to ensure availability.

SING ALONG AT FEINSTEIN'S
AT HOTEL CARMICHAEL

The upscale cabaret at the Hotel Carmichael is a one-stop shop for date night, featuring dinner and drinks alongside intimate musical performances. The venue also hosts comedy nights, murder mystery parties, and Broadway sing-alongs. And once a month, Feinstein's becomes a dueling piano bar, where attendees pick the playlist and sing along. The crowd skews a bit older—expect lots of Elton John, Billy Joel, and tunes from Woodstock. But the pianists also play more recent hits alongside crowd favorites like "Don't Stop Believin'" and university fight songs. (Just prepare to be booed if you request Taylor Swift.) Reservations are essential, so check the calendar for upcoming shows.

1 Carmichael Square, Carmel, 317-688-1947
feinsteinshc.com

LIGHT UP YOUR HOLIDAYS

AT WINTERLIGHTS

Since 2017, the Indianapolis Museum of Art at Newfields has hosted Winterlights, stringing up nearly two million Christmas lights in stunning displays throughout its parklike grounds. The highlight is the Landscape of Light, a sprawling lawn of light displays choreographed to music from *The Nutcracker*. When you need to warm up, cozy up to a bonfire with a hot chocolate or apple cider—spiked if you wish. Food options include s'mores kits and gingerbread popcorn. Winterlights also offers a peek into the historic Lilly House while it is lavishly decorated for the holidays.

4000 Michigan Rd., 317-923-1331
discovernewfields.org

TIP

Modeled on the holiday markets of Germany, the annual Carmel Christkindlmarkt features German food and drink, handmade goods, and an outdoor ice rink. You'll also find live music, artisan demonstrations, and a craft corner for children.

carmelchristkindlmarkt.com

42

HEAR THE MIDWEST'S BEST BLUES
AT THE SLIPPERY NOODLE INN

Founded in 1850, the Slippery Noodle Inn is Indiana's oldest bar and oldest surviving commercial building. In its early years, the Noodle may have served as a waystation on the Underground Railroad. During Prohibition, the owners made bootleg alcohol in the basement, and John Dillinger's gang used the stable for target practice. These days, however, the Noodle is one of the best venues in the Midwest for live blues. Come on Wednesdays for the popular open-stage blues jam, or stop by on weekends to see bands like the Why Store, the Warrior Kings, and the Gordon Bonham Blues Band. The bar has two stages, so you'll often get two shows for the price of one cover charge.

372 S Meridian St., 317-631-6974
slipperynoodle.com

GET TUNED UP
AT INDY'S JAZZ CLUBS

The Slippery Noodle Inn's stellar blues lineup may get all the press, but jazz fans in Indy have some other great options too, including Chatterbox Jazz on Mass Ave and the Jazz Kitchen in SoBro. Both have been around for decades, and both offer a mix of big-name performances and casual jam sessions. The Jazz Kitchen is a larger, more upscale venue, with a full menu of dishes inspired by Cajun and Creole cuisine. But the cozy little Chatterbox makes for intimate performances, and it's worth a stop just to read the extensive bathroom graffiti. The Chatterbox menu is limited, but it balances the scales by serving delicious meat pies from Patties of Jamaica—one of Indy's best-kept foodie secrets. If you have to choose just one, it's a toss-up, so check the performance calendars to see which lineup appeals to you more.

Chatterbox Jazz
435 Massachusetts Ave., 317-636-0584
chatterboxjazz.com

The Jazz Kitchen
5377 N College Ave., 317-253-4900
thejazzkitchen.com

PICNIC WITH MOZART
AT SYMPHONY ON THE PRAIRIE

For most of the year, the Indianapolis Symphony Orchestra performs in the Hilbert Circle Theatre on Monument Circle. But in the summer, the city's most talented classical musicians head north to the suburb of Fishers, where they perform in an outdoor amphitheater at Conner Prairie. Set against a beautiful backdrop of sunsets and starry nights, the Symphony on the Prairie series highlights a wide range of music, from Beethoven symphonies to Beatles hits. All you need is a picnic basket, a blanket, and a bottle of wine.

13400 Allisonville Rd., Fishers, 317-639-4300
indianapolissymphony.org

TIP

Little ones will love the Indianapolis Symphony Orchestra's Teddy Bear Concert Series. Designed for children ages 3 to 7, the 30-minute performances include storytelling, movement, and of course live music.

Courtesy of the Indianapolis Symphony Orchestra

45

FIND YOUR POLKA GROOVE
AT THE RATHSKELLER

The Rathskeller opened its doors in 1894 inside the Athenaeum, a social club for German immigrants. Now it's the city's oldest restaurant, and it still celebrates its Deutschland roots. It serves a hearty beer list and all the foods you'd find in a Munich beer hall: bratwurst, sauerbraten, schnitzel, and sauerkraut. But the best part is the biergarten, which is one of the city's best outdoor venues for live music. If you see just one band here, it should be the PolKatz. The local favorite adds a polka twist to classic tunes like "Don't Stop Believin'" and "Sweet Caroline."

401 E Michigan St., 317-636-0396
rathskeller.com

SEE THE BEST OF MODERN DANCE
AT DANCE KALEIDOSCOPE

If you enjoy TV shows like *So You Think You Can Dance*, you'll love Dance Kaleidoscope. It's the state's oldest professional dance company specializing in contemporary dance, and it consistently brings new ideas to the stage. The troupe performs at both the Indiana Repertory Theatre and the Tobias Theater at Newfields, and its musical selections range from classical music and jazz standards to Broadway favorites and recent pop hits. Dance Kaleidoscope also appears at community arts festivals; it often offers up one of my favorite performances at the IndyFringe Festival. One year its choreography, set to Tchaikovsky's *Romeo and Juliet*, actually left me in tears, and not just because I'm a Shakespeare geek.

317-419-2380
dancekal.org

Coach Nora at Cirque Indy
Courtesy of Peter M. Michael, In Dancing Light Photography

SPORTS AND RECREATION

47

GET SOME AERIAL EXERCISE

AT CIRQUE INDY

Indy has plenty of fitness options, from indoor gyms to outdoor trails. But even hardcore fitness buffs can get stuck in a rut, making exercise feel like a chore. Fortunately, Cirque Indy can break up the routine . . . by teaching you a new routine fit for a circus. Billing itself as "Indy's original circus school," the gym offers classes for all skill levels that incorporate aerial silks, hoops, slings, and static trapeze. Cirque Indy also offers youth classes and summer camps. Sessions are $30 each, but package discounts and monthly memberships are available.

617 N Fulton St., 317-758-7455
cirqueindy.com

KAYAK THE WHITE RIVER

WITH FRANK'S LIVERY

"You don't think of Indianapolis as a river city," said a guide at Frank's Paddlesports Livery one recent Saturday. And it's true that the White River was a disappointment to city founders who hoped to create a busy port. The river may not be navigable for cruise and cargo ships, but smaller boats are a different story. Founded in 2023, Frank's rents kayaks, canoes, and stand-up paddleboards, and it also arranges trips down the river. You'll begin at the facility next to Riverside Park, then be driven upriver to the launch point—Broad Ripple for a seven-mile adventure or Rocky Ripple for a four-mile outing. The trips are suitable for beginners, and the journey feels worlds away from the city. You can look for wildlife, have a picnic on a beach, and relax on a gentle river that feels like a secret.

3001 N White River Pkwy. Dr. W, 260-226-3075
frankslivery.com

FALL HARD FOR CURLING
WITH THE CIRCLE CITY CURLING CLUB

Watching curling during the Winter Olympics can be bewildering: Why, for example, are people sweeping the ice with brooms? What's all this talk about "ends" and "stones"? You'll get answers—and hands-on experience—at the Circle City Curling Club's Learn to Curl clinics. Each session includes 20 minutes of classroom time, where you'll hear about the rules and safety procedures (including how to fall correctly). Then, out on the ice, you'll learn how to launch stones, sweep, score, and strategize, and you'll put those skills to use in a mini-match with other beginners. Trust me, it's harder than it looks on TV, but don't worry about looking foolish. Yes, you will fall—but so will everyone else. And if you fall in love with curling, the club has leagues for players of all skill levels.

circlecitycurling.com

BE A PINHEAD AT DUCKPIN BOWLING

IN FOUNTAIN SQUARE

Duckpin bowling is primarily an East Coast pastime, and it reached its peak of popularity way back in the 1920s. But Fountain Square Theatre gives you the chance to try this scaled-back version of bowling, which uses smaller pins and grapefruit-sized balls. Scoring works the same way, but in duckpin bowling you get three balls per turn instead of two. The building offers two distinct experiences: Action Bowl has a 1930s art deco feel, while Atomic Bowl has a retro midcentury vibe. Reservations are essential for both bowling alleys, especially on weekends.

1105 Prospect St., 317-686-6010
fountainsquareindy.com

51

FIND SOME OLD-SCHOOL FUN
AT PINS MECHANICAL COMPANY

You could spend a whole day—or a whole staycation weekend—in the Bottleworks District without once leaving the premises. The district has its own hotel, a movie theater, a day spa, and dozens of food options, along with the massive Pins Mechanical Company entertainment complex. The facility has a full bar and specializes in "old-school entertainment," including 12 lanes for duckpin bowling, which it calls "the cooler, edgier cousin of traditional bowling." You'll also find vintage pinball machines, ping-pong and foosball tables, giant Jenga, indoor bocce courts, and hookie (think darts, but with rings that hook onto the target). It's fun for the whole family until 9 p.m., when the facility becomes an adults-only venue. Note that the venue doesn't offer reservations; all activities are first come, first served.

856 Carrollton Ave., 463-600-9100
bottleworksdistrict.com
pinsbar.com/locations/indianapolis

EXPLORE INDY BY BIKE

ON THE INDIANAPOLIS CULTURAL TRAIL

There's nothing in the world quite like the Indianapolis Cultural Trail. The eight-mile cycling and pedestrian path is a "linear park" connecting six downtown cultural districts: Fountain Square, Indiana Avenue, the Wholesale District, Market East, White River State Park, and Mass Ave. The trail also links to Broad Ripple via the Monon Trail. No bike? No problem. The city's bike-share program has 25 rental stations across the city, and you can purchase either a day pass or an annual membership.

indyculturaltrail.org
pacersbikeshare.org

TIP

Public artwork abounds on the Indianapolis Cultural Trail. Tucked away on the 700 block of Mass Ave, for example, is a unique piece, *Chatham Passage*. The conceptual artwork by Sean Derry features an underground machine that spreads the scent of roses. It's hard to spot visually, so follow your nose.

53

GO PADDLING
AT EAGLE CREEK PARK

Eagle Creek Park is the largest park in the city and one of the largest city parks in the nation. Its amenities include a beach and marina, a dog park, several nature centers, hiking trails, and the Go Ape Zipline & Adventure Park. The park's Eagle Creek Outfitters rents out canoes, stand-up paddleboards, kayaks, pontoon boats, and sailboats. But don't overlook its guided paddle programs, where you'll kayak or canoe with a tour guide and hear interesting stories about the park and its animal inhabitants. Book early for sunset tours, which are offered only when the moon is full.

7840 W 56th St., 317-327-7110
indy.gov/eaglecreek

TIP

At the GoApe Zipline & Adventure Park, start with the Treetop Adventure course. The "ultimate outdoor challenge" includes ziplines, rope bridges, and Tarzan swings, as well as challenging airborne obstacles. Just note that the course has a minimum age requirement of 10 years.

54

STOP AND SMELL THE ROSES
AT INDY'S PRETTIEST GARDENS

When you need respite from the hustle and bustle, seek refuge in one of the city's beautiful gardens. On the south side of town, the 10,000-square-foot Garfield Park Conservatory offers a year-round display of tropical plants, and the park's Sunken Garden mimics the formal gardens of Europe. Downtown, the Indianapolis Zoo's White River Gardens is a three-acre botanical garden best known for its spring tulips. Each summer, White River Gardens fills its 5,000-square-foot conservatory with thousands of butterflies, including rare species from across the globe. On the north side, Butler University's campus is home to Holcomb Gardens, a 20-acre swath of woodlands and formal gardens. Bring a picnic blanket and sprawl near the statue of Persephone, the Greek goddess whose annual return from the underworld heralds the arrival of spring.

Garfield Park Conservatory and Sunken Garden
2505 Conservatory Dr., 317-327-7183
garfieldgardensconservatory.org

Holcomb Gardens
4600 Sunset Ave.
800-368-6852
butler.edu

White River Gardens
1200 W Washington St.
317-630-2001
indianapoliszoo.com

SEE BASEBALL UP CLOSE
WITH THE INDIANAPOLIS INDIANS

You can root, root, root for the home team at Victory Field, where cheering for the minor league Indianapolis Indians is like stepping back in time. The tickets are affordable, the stadium is small, and the concession stands still serve peanuts and Cracker Jack.

Victory Field is part of downtown's White River State Park, and it offers a spectacular view of the city skyline—especially in the summer, when games on Friday evenings are followed by a free fireworks show. No wonder *Sports Illustrated* dubbed it "the best minor league ballpark in the nation."

Looking for a bargain? Sign up the kiddos for the Knot Hole Kids Club. Membership includes free game tickets and a chance to run the bases after Sunday home games.

501 W Maryland St., 317-269-3542
indyindians.com

JOIN THE SOCCER CRAZE
WITH THE INDY ELEVEN

My late father-in-law used to joke that soccer was the sport of the future . . . and always would be. Fans of the Indy Eleven would beg to differ. Indy's professional soccer team was founded in 2013 and rapidly built its fan base, becoming the first team in the history of the North American Soccer League to sell out every home game of its inaugural season. The Indy Eleven play home games at the Michael A. Carroll Track and Soccer Stadium, but the team has big plans for a venue of its own. Tickets start at an affordable $15, so come see the sport of the future, today.

indyeleven.com

TIP

Another local team to watch is Indy Ignite, which played its inaugural season in 2025. The women's professional volleyball team is based at the Fishers Event Center.

provolleyball.com/teams/indy-ignite

57

GO TO A COLTS GAME
AT LUCAS OIL STADIUM

Indiana is basketball territory, but Indy residents love their football team, too. The NFL's Indianapolis Colts play at Lucas Oil Stadium, which opened in 2008 to replace the antiquated RCA Dome. The stadium seats 67,000 fans and offers a great view of the downtown skyline, so seeing a football game here is an essential Indy experience, even if you're not much of a sports fan.

Can't make it to a game? Sign up instead for a behind-the-scenes stadium tour, which includes visits to the playing field, locker room, and press box. Tours are offered every Friday at 11 a.m., 1 p.m., and 3 p.m.

500 S Capitol Ave., 317-262-8600
lucasoilstadium.com

RUN THE RACETRACK
AT THE MINI-MARATHON

Each May, the 500 Festival kicks off its month-long celebration with the Mini-Marathon, one of the nation's largest half marathons. Even with 35,000 slots, it often sells out months in advance. What's the appeal? Perhaps it's that the route includes a 2.5-mile loop around the Indianapolis Motor Speedway—which counts as hallowed ground in Indianapolis. The Mini-Marathon also comes at just the right time to serve as a motivational goal for runners who start training because of New Year's resolutions.

indymini.com

TIP

Check the schedule for Mini weekend, which also includes shakeout and recovery runs and the two-day Mini-Marathon Expo at Lucas Oil Stadium.

EXPERIENCE THE GREATEST SPECTACLE IN RACING: THE INDIANAPOLIS 500

Without seeing the Indianapolis Motor Speedway in person, it's hard to comprehend the scale of the world's largest venue for spectator sports. Constructed in 1909, the facility encloses a 2.5-mile oval track and can seat a quarter of a million race fans.

Since 1911, the speedway's signature event has been the Indianapolis 500, where 33 of the world's top INDYCAR drivers compete at speeds of up to 237 miles per hour. Held annually on the Sunday before Memorial Day, the "greatest spectacle in racing" is steeped in tradition, such as singing "Back Home Again in Indiana" before the race and watching the winner quench his—and someday her—thirst with a glass bottle of milk.

4790 W 16th St., 317-492-6700
indianapolismotorspeedway.com

TIP

Book a seat in turn one, where you'll have the best view of the finish line, the pits, and all the risky racing action. And bring a radio scanner, which lets you eavesdrop on the drivers and their pit crews.

GO BEYOND THE FINISH LINE

The Indianapolis 500 happens just once a year, but Indy celebrates its racing culture year-round. To explore the history of the race, head to the Indianapolis Motor Speedway Museum on the speedway grounds. The museum, which recently got a major overhaul, has interactive exhibits describing advances in racing safety and speed. The museum also has a large collection of race cars, including the Marmon Wasp that won the inaugural Indy 500 in 1911. It is interesting to see how the cars have evolved over time. For an additional fee, you can take a guided tour around the track itself.

4750 W 16th St., 463-244-2680
imsmuseum.org

TIP

Hungry in Speedway? Head to Borage, a neighborhood café, bakery, and market serving all-day breakfast, weekend brunch, and a surprisingly elevated dinner menu.

1609 N Lynhurst Dr., 317-734-3958, borageeats.com

61

EXPERIENCE INDIANA BASKETBALL

The old saying is true: In 49 states it's just basketball, but this is Indiana. If you count how many homes have basketball hoops in the driveway, you'll begin to understand the intensity of Hoosiers' passion. To deepen that understanding, watch *Hoosiers*. It's a true Cinderella story about a high school team from tiny Milan, Indiana, that goes on (spoiler alert) to win the state basketball championship.

Now you're ready for some games. Indy is home to the NBA's Indiana Pacers and the WNBA's Indiana Fever, both of which play at Gainbridge Fieldhouse. College hoops get you closer to the action, so watch the Butler University Bulldogs play at Indy's historic Hinkle Fieldhouse. And, as *Hoosiers* suggests, high school is the true heart of Hoosier basketball, so pick a Friday night and go cheer for your neighborhood team.

Butler University Bulldogs
butlersports.com

Indiana Fever
wnba.com/fever

Indiana Pacers
nba.com/pacers

Glassblowing classes at Glass Arts Indiana
Courtesy of Factory Arts District

CULTURE AND HISTORY

CELEBRATE FIRST FRIDAY
AT THE FACTORY ARTS DISTRICT

These days, the First Friday energy is in the Factory Arts District, which bills itself as "an ungentrified, unpretentious, uncommonly interesting place." Formerly known as the Circle City Industrial Complex, the district is anchored by Centerpoint Brewing Company. The rough-around-the-edges Factory Arts North building is home to more than 120 artists' studios, featuring everything from paintings and fine art prints to jewelry, photography, fused glass, clothing, custom lighting, and stuffed animals. The art is surprisingly affordable; on a recent First Friday, I purchased a vibrant painting of the Soldiers and Sailors Monument for just $65. Stay tuned for further developments in the Factory Arts South building, currently in the planning stages.

1125 Brookside Ave., 317-801-3612
factoryartsdistrict.com

63

EXPLORE INDIANA AVENUE
WITH THROUGH2EYES

Indiana Avenue was once the "Main Street" of a vibrant black community. But because of interstate construction, IUPUI expansion, and other factors, not much remains of the old neighborhood. On his "walk and talk" tours of the area, Sampson Levingston of Through2Eyes brings the neighborhood back to life, using historical maps, books, and photographs to help customers visualize what we've lost. Two-hour tours start at the Indianapolis Urban League and cover about two miles. Sampson also offers historical tours of other Circle City neighborhoods, including Irvington, Butler-Tarkington, Martindale, and Haughville.

through2eyes.com/walk-talk

HIT THE ROOF
AT THE HARRISON CENTER

Located on the Near Northside, the Harrison Center is home to eight art galleries and about 30 artist studios—all of which come to life on First Fridays. You can take the yellow slide to the lower-level galleries or ride the karaoke elevator to the rooftop patio, where you can mingle with fellow art lovers and get a breath of fresh air. The Harrison Center shares the building with ArtMix, an arts program for people with disabilities, and samples of the artists' works line the hallways. If you want to explore the building outside of First Fridays hours, visit the website in advance to book a free guided tour.

1505 N Delaware St., 317-396-3886
harrisoncenter.org

TIP

Another First Friday favorite is the Tube Factory Artspace in Garfield Park, managed by the Big Car Collaborative. The campus includes an art gallery with rotating exhibitions, as well as a bee sanctuary, coffeeshop, and housing for local artists.

1125 S Cruft St., 317-450-6630, tubefactory.org

GO HUNTING FOR GHOSTS
WITH UNSEEN PRESS

The Athenaeum on Mass Ave started its life in the 1890s as Das Deutsche Haus, a community center for Indianapolis's German immigrants. And it still houses the Rathskeller, the oldest restaurant in Indianapolis. No doubt the building has many tales to tell—including more than a few ghost stories. Local tour company Unseen Press conducts overnight paranormal investigations in the building, encouraging attendees to bring EMF meters, digital voice recorders, cameras, and other equipment to track down evidence of ghosts. Don't believe in ghosts? I didn't either—until I spent a night at the Athenaeum. Even if you're not into ghosts, you'll get to see areas of the historic building that are off-limits to daytime visitors.

unseenpress.com

TIP

Unseen Press also offers guided ghost walks through downtown Indianapolis, Westfield, and Noblesville. Check the calendar for upcoming events.

SLEEP IN A HISTORIC PULLMAN CAR

AT UNION STATION

In the 1800s, Indianapolis was the first city in the nation to create a centralized passenger train station for the many railroad companies operating in the area at the time. The Union Depot was built first, then the much larger and grander Union Station, which was completed in 1888. But in recent decades, with the decline in passenger train traffic, the station has been repurposed. It is now home to the Crowne Plaza hotel, which offers a unique overnight option: 26 guest suites in authentic early 1900s Pullman train cars, still sitting on the original tracks. The hotel also has traditional guest rooms, as well as two restaurants and—maybe—a couple of ghosts.

123 W Louisiana St., 317-631-2221
ihg.com

FIGURE OUT A THEATER SCHEDULE
AT THE INDYFRINGE FESTIVAL

To understand the magic of the IndyFringe Festival each August, you have to do some math: six different stages in four theater venues + 10 days + 70 unique shows = more than 250 performances to choose from. The hard part is setting your schedule. In one day, you can see a wacky new musical about bowling pins, a reinterpretation of a Shakespearean classic, a family-friendly magic show, a raunchy stand-up comedy act, a dance performance, and a choral concert. You may encounter a few clunkers along the way, but even those are sure to be memorable. Tickets start at $22, but the festival offers package deals and discounted last-minute tickets.

719 E St. Clair St., 317-210-4639
indyfringe.org

TIP

The IF Theatre does more than host an annual festival; it's a year-round destination for contemporary, offbeat, and experimental shows. Check the calendar for upcoming events.

68

SIGHTSEE ON MONUMENT CIRCLE
WITH INDIANA LANDMARKS

The heart of Indianapolis is Monument Circle, from which the city derives its Circle City nickname. You can learn more about the history and architecture of the circle on an informative walking tour with Indiana Landmarks, an organization focused on historic preservation. Whether you're a visitor or a local, you'll discover many secrets hidden in plain sight. Tours depart from Christ Church Cathedral and cover about half a mile. The organization also offers walking tours of White River State Park and several historic downtown neighborhoods.

317-639-4534
indianalandmarks.org

FOUR MORE REASONS TO VISIT MONUMENT CIRCLE

1. The annual Circle of Lights tree-lighting ceremony, which transforms the Soldiers and Sailors Monument into the world's tallest Christmas tree.

2. The annual Strawberry Festival, at which Christ Church Cathedral dishes up six tons of strawberries and more than 18,000 homemade shortcakes.

3. The Indianapolis Symphony Orchestra, which performs at Monument Circle's historic Hilbert Circle Theatre.

4. Organ and choral concerts at Christ Church Cathedral.

TAKE A CREATIVE CLASS
AT THE INDY ART CENTER

The Indianapolis Art Center is one of the best places in town to develop a new creative skill. The center has large studios for glassblowing, welding, and woodworking, and its instructors excel at teaching painting, photography, drawing, ceramics, jewelry-making, weaving, and other skills. Plunge in with a university-style class that spans up to 15 weeks, giving you a chance to create multiple projects. Not ready to commit? Try a weekend workshop or a two-hour pop-up class focused on a specific project, such as a glass paperweight or metal bracelet. The Art Center also has classes for children and teenagers, including weeklong summer camps.

820 E 67th St., 317-255-2464
indplsartcenter.org

TIP

The juried Broad Ripple Art Fair, held each May on the campus of the Indianapolis Art Center, showcases the region's best artists and artisans in a fun atmosphere, complete with live music and beer tastings.

MORE ARTSY ADVENTURES

Art classes abound in Indianapolis. Here are a few more to try.

Create Art Studio

Adult classes at this cute Broad Ripple cottage cover topics such as embroidery, knitting, painting, sketching, candle-making, flower arranging, and jewelry. The studio also has classes and parties for children and teens.

6511 Ferguson St., 317-469-1309
createartstudioindy.com

Fountain Square Clay Center

Start with a two-hour evening class, where you'll learn the basics of wheel-throwing and make one or two pots of your own. If you love it, the center offers eight-week classes in wheel-throwing and hand-building for multiple skill levels.

950 Hosbrook St., 317-985-1212
fountainsquareclaycenter.com

Glass Arts Indiana

Tucked away in the maze of the Factory Arts District, Glass Arts Indiana has dozens of class options for both blown and fused glass. Make a paperweight, suncatcher, or drinking glass, or even a tiny glass chicken. Private lessons are also available.

1125 Brookside Ave., Ste. C-25, 317-744-0010
glassartsindiana.org

SEE THE STARS
AT THE HOLCOMB OBSERVATORY AND PLANETARIUM

When night falls on the campus of Butler University, the domed tower of Holcomb Observatory casts a gentle glow across the quiet lawns. Constructed in 1954, the observatory is open for public tours on many weekend evenings during the school year. There's no charge to gaze through Indiana's largest telescope, which recently underwent a $425,000 refurbishment. Tour guides, who are usually astronomy students, point out such objects as planets, the moon, and star clusters. The supplementary planetarium show costs just $8. In other words, it's one of the cheapest dates in town. Just keep an eye on the weather forecast. Viewings are canceled when heavy cloud cover limits visibility.

4600 Sunset Ave., 317-940-8333
butler.edu/holcomb-observatory

71

PICNIC AT THE RUINS
AT HOLLIDAY PARK

Encompassing 94 acres, Holliday Park offers the usual mix of playgrounds, picnic areas, and walking trails. But it does have one unique feature, the Ruins, which makes you feel like you're picnicking in Athens or Rome. Its three large sculptures, called *The Races of Man*, were rescued from the facade of New York's St. Paul Building before its demolition in the 1950s. The building's owner wanted to save the statues, which were then valued at about $150,000. So it held a design competition, asking cities to submit proposals for putting the statues on permanent display. Indy's winning plan mimicked the facade of the St. Paul Building, thus placing the statues in their original context. In the end, it was something of a homecoming for the statues, which were carved from Indiana limestone. Pack a picnic basket and go say hello.

6363 Spring Mill Rd., 317-327-7180
hollidaypark.org

TIP

Holliday Park's Rock the Ruins summer concert series brings in surprisingly big names with reasonable ticket prices. Check the calendar for details.

rocktheruins.com

TAKE A GRAVEYARD TOUR
AT CROWN HILL CEMETERY

Crown Hill Cemetery, which opened in 1864, is the third-largest nongovernmental cemetery in the nation. It's the final resting place of more than 200,000 people, including Depression-era bank robber John Dillinger, President Benjamin Harrison, poet James Whitcomb Riley, and novelist Booth Tarkington. Riley's monument is a perfect spot for a sunset picnic; it sits atop the highest hill in Marion County, offering a great view of the downtown skyline.

A guided tour is the best way to appreciate Crown Hill. Start with the two-hour Skeletons in the Closet tour to get the dirt on Crown Hill residents. The cemetery also offers fall foliage tours and walks focused on Civil War history and Victorian tombstone symbolism.

700 W 38th St., 317-920-4165
crownhillhf.org/tours-events/public-tours

73

WANDER THE VIRGINIA B. FAIRBANKS ART & NATURE PARK

Just west of the Indianapolis Museum of Art at Newfields is its 100-acre outdoor sculpture gallery, the Virginia B. Fairbanks Art & Nature Park. Perhaps the best-known artwork in the park is a giant skeleton called *Funky Bones*, which features in the novel *The Fault in Our Stars* by Indianapolis writer John Green. Kids often have a great time jumping from bone to bone; the artworks here are meant to be interactive. The surreal basketball court *Free Basket* is visible from the road. Another sculpture, *Oracle of Intimation*, looks like the roof of a house that has been buried underground. And *Park of the Laments* is a hidden garden within a garden, creating a quiet and contemplative space. Even the bright yellow benches throughout the park are works of art—but don't worry, it's still okay to sit on them.

1850 W 38th St.
discovernewfields.org/art-in-the-park

EXPLORE THE DESIGN GALLERY

AT THE INDIANAPOLIS MUSEUM OF ART

When you hear the phrase "art museum," you might think of ancient Greek statues and European Renaissance paintings. The Indianapolis Museum of Art at Newfields has those things, but it also has something unexpected. Its 11,000-square-foot Design Gallery is the largest of its kind in the country, featuring contemporary household items such as furniture, typewriters, teapots, lamps, appliances, and clocks—all with a special artsy twist. My favorite piece is *You Can't Lay Down Your Memories*, a wonky cabinet made of freestanding drawers. Wandering the gallery, you'll feel inspired to seek out more artful designs for your own home.

4000 Michigan Rd., 317-923-1331
discovernewfields.org

THE PENROD ARTS FAIR

In Indianapolis, the first Saturday after Labor Day is known as "Indiana's Nicest Day." The event is the annual Penrod Arts Fair, held at Newfields since 1967. It is one of the largest single-day art fairs in the nation, attracting about 350 artists and more than 20,000 attendees. Scattered throughout the grounds of the Indianapolis Museum of Art are a children's play area, multiple performance stages, dozens of food and drink vendors, and booths for about 50 local arts-related nonprofit organizations.

4000 Michigan Rd.
penrod.org

75

SEEK OUT INDY'S SPOOKY SIDE
WITH IRVINGTON GHOST TOURS

Located five miles east of downtown Indy, Irvington was the city's first suburb. Although the neighborhood was annexed back in 1902, its residents maintain a fierce sense of community pride. Looking for a fun way to explore the neighborhood's winding streets and Victorian architecture? Your best bet is Irvington Ghost Tours, which offers two-hour walking tours throughout October in conjunction with the neighborhood's fabulous Halloween festival. Guides share stories about John Dillinger, who robbed an Irvington drugstore before he robbed his first bank, and serial killer H. H. Holmes, of *Devil in the White City* fame.

But the ghost you should remember is Madge Oberholtzer. In 1925, the bright young woman was kidnapped, tortured, and murdered by D. C. Stephenson, the grand dragon of the state's Ku Klux Klan. Her deathbed statement led to Stephenson's conviction for murder and permanently crippled the KKK's hold on Indiana politics. Both of their homes are included on the tour.

317-850-1910
indianaghosttours.org

76

GET DRAMATIC
WITH INDY'S THEATER SCENE

In recent years, the Indy theater scene has stepped out of Chicago's long shadow. In addition to Indy Shakes and the IF Theatre, covered elsewhere in this book, there's the Phoenix Theatre. Formerly housed in an old church on Mass Ave, it recently moved to a purpose-built space on Illinois Street. It's best known for its hilarious Christmas show. But there's challenging drama here too, including *The Cripple of Inishmaan* and *August: Osage County*. For a more consistently straitlaced production, try the Indiana Repertory Theatre. Recent shows have included *Little Shop of Horror*s and *The Glass Menagerie*, and its annual production of *A Christmas Carol* is a holiday tradition for many families.

Indiana Repertory Theatre
140 W Washington St., 317-635-5252
irtlive.com

Phoenix Theatre
705 N Illinois St., 317-635-7529
phoenixtheatre.org

77

SEE SHAKESPEARE
UNDER THE STARS

Quality productions of Shakespeare's plays can be hard to come by in Indy, so Indy Shakes is a breath of fresh air. Each summer, the company's professional actors mount a Shakespeare production, such as *Othello* or *As You Like It*, in a local park. The actors take their work seriously, but the atmosphere is casual: picnicking is encouraged, admission is free, and families are welcome—as are Comic Con attendees still wearing their Pokémon costumes (true story). On surveys, many attendees report that they've never seen any play before, let alone a Shakespeare play, but the talented actors can ease even the most reluctant playgoers into the rhythm of Shakespeare's language. The magic of Indy Shakes is that it trusts its audiences to rise to the challenge—and, year after year, they do.

indyshakes.com

GO WILD
AT THE INDIANAPOLIS ZOO

You can take a trip around the world at the Indianapolis Zoo, which is home to more than 250 animal species. One highlight is the International Orangutan Center: the aerial environment houses nine orangutans, giving them plenty of space to climb. Flights of Fancy consists of three walk-through aviaries, including one where you can feed birdseed to colorful budgies. The Oceans exhibit also has interactive options, including a shark-petting tank and lively dolphin shows. (If you plan ahead, you can schedule a time to swim with the dolphins.) The Deserts Dome is home to meerkats and lizards, and the Forests Biome houses tigers, lemurs, and bears. The largest section is the Plains Biome, where you'll find African animals, such as zebras, giraffes, rhinos, cheetahs, lions, and elephants.

1200 W Washington St., 317-630-2001
indianapoliszoo.com

RIDE A HISTORIC CAROUSEL
AT THE CHILDREN'S MUSEUM OF INDIANAPOLIS

The world's largest children's museum is a wonderland of dinosaurs, trains, mummies, carnival rides, and much more. In the Dinosphere exhibit, an immersive environment brings to life the sounds, smells, and sights of the dinosaur era. In ScienceWorks, kids can race boats down an indoor creek and climb aboard construction equipment. In Treasures of the Earth, visitors can reconstruct an Egyptian mummy or a Chinese terra-cotta warrior. The museum also has a planetarium, a huge play area for babies and toddlers, outdoor sports experiences, and a stunning five-story glass sculpture by artist Dale Chihuly.

But the best spot is the Carousel Wishes and Dreams exhibit, which is home to a restored 1917 carousel you can actually ride. The exhibit also has funhouse mirrors and mazes, a treehouse, and vintage video games. You'll get the kids to leave only by promising them a visit to the enormous gift shop on the way out.

3000 N Meridian St., 317-334-4000
childrensmuseum.org

80

STEP INTO HISTORY
AT CONNER PRAIRIE

It's always 1836 in Prairie Town, the centerpiece of the Conner Prairie living history museum in Fishers. The outdoor village is populated by costumed interpreters who welcome visitors to pioneer homes, a schoolhouse, a general store, and an inn. Along the way, you can watch demonstrations of traditional crafts like pottery, carpentry, and blacksmithing; visit with the farm animals; and perhaps even watch an old-fashioned baseball game. The property is also home to the historic William Conner House, a re-created Lenape village, and a tethered hot-air balloon that ascends 370 feet into the sky (yes, you can ride it). In addition, watch the calendar for special events, such as cooking classes, cocktail tastings, and guided nature hikes.

13400 Allisonville Rd., Fishers, 317-776-6000
connerprairie.org

81

EXPLORE INDY'S MUSEUM CAMPUS

White River State Park is a scenic spot for a picnic, but it's also home to several popular museums. Start your museum-hopping day at the Indiana State Museum, which highlights the state's natural and cultural history. Let yourself be mesmerized by the gentle swing of the Foucault pendulum, which demonstrates the Earth's rotation, and then look for sculptures from all 92 Indiana counties embedded in the museum's facade and walkways. Nearby is the Eiteljorg Museum of American Indians and Western Art, which has one of the world's top collections of contemporary Native American art. Finally, head to the NCAA Hall of Champions, which celebrates collegiate sports with two floors of interactive exhibits and video highlights. White River State Park is also home to the Indianapolis Zoo and Victory Field.

Eiteljorg Museum of American Indians and Western Art
500 W Washington St., 317-636-9378
eiteljorg.org

Indiana State Museum
650 W Washington St., 317-232-1637
indianamuseum.org

NCAA Hall of Champions
700 W Washington St., 317-916-4255
ncaahallofchampions.org

COMMUNE WITH KILGORE TROUT

AT THE KURT VONNEGUT MUSEUM AND LIBRARY

The late author Kurt Vonnegut said, "All my jokes are Indianapolis. All my attitudes are Indianapolis. . . . If I ever severed myself from Indianapolis, I would be out of business." The Kurt Vonnegut Museum and Library celebrates the hometown author and his numerous books, such as *Slaughterhouse-Five*, *Cat's Cradle*, *Breakfast of Champions*, and *The Sirens of Titan*. The three-story facility displays many pieces of Vonnegut memorabilia, including his typewriter, eyeglasses, and collection of rejection letters. The third floor focuses on Vonnegut's experience as a prisoner of war during the firebombing of Dresden, Germany, in WWII. Try to schedule your visit around the guided tour offered daily at noon (1 p.m. on Sundays) to gain deeper insight into the permanent and temporary exhibits.

543 Indiana Ave., 317-423-0391
vonnegutlibrary.org

83

CELEBRATE AFRICAN AMERICAN CULTURE
AT INDIANA BLACK EXPO'S SUMMER CELEBRATION

Held each July, Indiana Black Expo's Summer Celebration is the state's premier showcase of African American culture and one of the largest festivals of ethnic culture in the nation. The 10-day schedule includes concerts, fashion shows, and an enormous exhibition hall, where vendors sell everything from hair-care products to health insurance. The Summer Celebration also includes community-focused events, such as health fairs and educational workshops. Can't make it to the Summer Celebration? Mark your calendar instead for IBE's Circle City Classic. The annual fall football game highlights teams from two historically black colleges or universities.

indianablackexpo.com

SEE A TRULY MOVING PICTURE
AT THE HEARTLAND INTERNATIONAL FILM FESTIVAL

It's not quite Cannes, but each October the Heartland International Film Festival brings together independent filmmakers from across the globe. Over a 10-day period, the festival offers public screenings of about 120 films, which is less than 10 percent of the films submitted to the festival for consideration. The festival's reputation for feel-good films isn't quite accurate; its real focus is "purposeful" filmmaking that educates and inspires, not just entertains. You might see documentaries about Indigenous wrestlers, black farmers, drag queens, Ukrainian artists, or pickleball; fictional features about love and loss; or an animated film about a woman who hoards snails. And you might meet some of the world's top filmmakers along the way.

8950 Otis Ave., 317-464-9405
heartlandfilm.org/festival

85

PAY HOMAGE
AT INDY'S WAR MEMORIALS

Fun fact: Washington, DC, is the only city in the nation with more war memorials than Indianapolis. One highlight is the Indiana War Memorial Plaza, a cluster of neoclassical monuments honoring local veterans of World War II, the Vietnam War, and the Korean War. To the north and south, the plaza is bookended by the American Legion's national headquarters and the Indiana War Memorial, which houses a surprising military museum. Along the nearby Canal Walk, you'll find memorials to the USS *Indianapolis*, which was torpedoed in 1945, and to recipients of the Congressional Medal of Honor. And don't forget the Soldiers and Sailors Monument on Monument Circle; it honors veterans of earlier conflicts, including the Civil War.

HUNT FOR PUBLIC ART
WITH THE INDY ARTS COUNCIL

New murals, sculptures, and other pieces of public art are appearing all over Indianapolis, making it hard to keep track of individual pieces. Fortunately, the Indy Arts Council maintains an online directory of public art throughout the city. Peruse the list, then head out into the city to discover your favorites.

You'll find several iconic pieces along Mass Ave. Julian Opie's *Ann Dancing* is an electronic sign featuring a swaying female figure. Nearby is James Tyler's *Brick Head 3*, a large human head made of bricks. And you can't miss *My Affair with Kurt Vonnegut*, an enormous mural created by artist Pamela Bliss to memorialize the late hometown author.

My personal favorites are four cute sculptures by Tom Otterness, purchased after a temporary installation of his sculptures throughout the city in 2005. *Boy and Dog* resides at the corner of East and St. Clair Streets, just steps from Mass Ave. Three other pieces, *Free Money*, *Female Tourist*, and *Male Tourist*, live in front of the Indiana Convention Center.

indyarts.org/public-art-directory

DISCOVER THE HOOSIER PRESIDENT AT THE BENJAMIN HARRISON PRESIDENTIAL SITE

Although President Benjamin Harrison was born in Ohio, he spent his entire adult life as an attorney in the Circle City—with the exception of the four years he spent in Washington, DC. His 16-room Italianate Victorian mansion was built in 1874, and it was from this home that he conducted his famous "front porch campaign" for the presidency. The house, which recently underwent a $6 million renovation, displays more than 10,000 presidential artifacts, including Harrison's furniture, housewares, artwork, and political memorabilia. The third-floor ballroom houses changing exhibits. Guided tours are offered every day of the week, unless the site is booked for a special event.

1230 N Delaware St., 317-631-1888
bhpsite.org

TIP

When you reach Citizenship Plaza, look for "The Book of History." It honors more than 1,500 Americans who have become naturalized citizens on this site since 2003.

Courtesy of United State of Indiana

SHOPPING AND FASHION

WEAR YOUR HOMETOWN PRIDE
AT UNITED STATE OF INDIANA

Tucked away in SoBro is United State of Indiana, a shop that celebrates the Hoosier state. The specialty here is themed shirts. Some reference *Parks and Recreation* or *Stranger Things*, two popular TV series set in Indiana. Others highlight bygone cultural icons like the Tee Pee Restaurant and Hook's drugstore. One T-shirt covered in pictures of Hoosier agricultural products reads, "This is my crop top." In addition to clothing, the shop stocks magnets, stickers, coffee mugs, tote bags, pins, flags, and posters. The shop's motto: "Be kind. Be helpful. Be Hoosier."

1051 E 54th St.
unitedstateofindiana.com

TIP

Just down the street is Corridor, a food market known for its delicious Nicole-Taylor's fresh pasta. Pick up a bag with inventive shapes and flavors to cook at home.

89

BUY A PIECE OF HISTORY
AT PEOPLE FOR URBAN PROGRESS

The RCA Dome was demolished in 2008, but you can still buy a piece of its iconic 13-acre fabric roof. The nonprofit People for Urban Progress salvaged the Teflon-coated fiberglass, and ever since PUP has been churning out handbags, tote bags, and other accessories using that material. The organization also uses banners from bygone sporting events and seat covers from old Amtrak trains. Every piece is one of a kind, and proceeds go toward clever reuse initiatives: for example, using thousands of discarded seats from the late Bush Stadium to create seating areas at bus stops across the city. Stop by the small showroom near the former Central State Hospital to find your own unique and sustainable accessory—you might get an impromptu tour. PUP products are also available at gift shops around town, including Silver in the City and Speedway's Three Sisters and a Trunk.

160 Steeples Blvd., 317-497-5492
peopleup.org

90

TREAT YOURSELF
AT SILVER IN THE CITY

Silver in the City is an absolute delight, and it's impossible to leave the eclectic shop without buying something—or at least desperately wanting to. The right side of the Mass Ave store has affordable jewelry galore. On the left, the shop stocks cute housewares, clever books, and fun gift items, such as puzzles, party games, candles, coffee mugs, stationery, and sassy stickers. You'll quickly find something you can't live without, whether it's an axolotl figurine, a tin of emergency googly eyes, or a pasta-shaped hair clip. This is also one of the best places in the city to find gifts and souvenirs with an Indianapolis or Indiana theme.

434 Massachusetts Ave., 317-955-9925
silverinthecity.com

MEET HOOSIER ARTISANS
AT THE INDIANA ARTISAN MARKETPLACE

The Indiana Artisan program recognizes the state's top makers, from woodworkers to sculptors to cheesemakers. The juried program isn't just a rubber stamp for handmade goods; it's a seal of approval awarded to only a small fraction of the artisans who apply. The annual Indiana Artisan Marketplace, held each spring at the Indiana State Fairgrounds, showcases the work of more than 300 approved artisans. Shop for unique artwork, pretty paper goods, eye-catching jewelry, crave-worthy food products, and the state's best beers and wines. You won't find many bargains here. Instead, come prepared to splurge on a one-of-a-kind piece that you'll treasure for a lifetime.

indianaartisan.org

TIP

You can shop Indiana Artisan handicrafts year-round at the organization's showroom in the Carmel Arts & Design District.

22 N Rangeline Rd., 317-964-9455

92

SHOP MASS AVE

Silver in the City isn't the only reason to visit Mass Ave. The angled avenue is also home to clothing boutiques such as Sage and Francis + Fern, both located in the 400 block. Nearby are two bakeries: Three Dog Bakery for dog treats and the Flying Cupcake Bakery for human treats. (Don't miss the Red Velvet Elvis.) You'll find unique home decor and gift items at Artisans and, farther down the avenue, Decorate and Chatham Home. There's another cluster of shops in the 800 block. Penn & Beech enables customers to create their own scented candles. Global Gifts stocks fair trade items, while Goodies & Giggles sells toys, books, crafting kits, and games. Crimson Tate: Modern Quilter is a regional destination for fabrics. In addition, the 800 block houses Mass Ave Wine, the excellent Tomorrow Bookstore, and Vintage Kulture Clothing. Try combining your shopping trip with a meal at any of the excellent restaurants along the way.

Artisans
429 Massachusetts Ave.
317-744-5352, artisansindy.com

Chatham Home
517 E Walnut St., 317-917-8550
chathamhomeindy.com

Crimson Tate: Modern Quilter
845 Massachusetts Ave.
317-426-3300, crimsontate.com

Decorate
708 Massachusetts Ave.
317-737-2109, decorateindy.com

The Flying Cupcake
423 Massachusetts Ave.
317-396-2696
theflyingcupcakebakery.com

Francis + Fern
421 Massachusetts Ave.
317-643-1890
francisandfernboutique.com

Global Gifts

873 Massachusetts Ave., 317-423-3148
globalgiftsft.com

Goodies & Giggles Toy Store

811 Massachusetts Ave., 317-289-1226
goodiesandgiggles.com

Mass Ave Wine

878 Massachusetts Ave., 317-972-7966

Penn & Beech Candle Co.

820 Massachusetts Ave., 317-721-6885
pennandbeech.com

Sage Boutique

431 Massachusetts Ave., 317-423-2919

Silver in the City

434 Massachusetts Ave., 317-955-9925
silverinthecity.com

Three Dog Bakery

444 Massachusetts Ave., 317-238-0000
threedogindy.com

Tomorrow Bookstore

882 Massachusetts Ave., 317-551-1893
bookshop.org/shop/tomorrowbookstore

Vintage Kulture Clothing

867 Massachusetts Ave.
vtgkulture.com

SHOP FOUNTAIN SQUARE

In Fountain Square, the 1000 block of Virginia Avenue is anchored by Indy Reads, which has its own entry in this book. But other treasures await just down the block. Zodiac Vintage stocks vintage clothing, including a wide selection of jeans. Snakeroot Botanicals has any house plant you could want, along with pretty pots and basic gardening supplies. Rooftop Fruit sells forward-thinking toiletries and gift items, while Howl + Hide specializes in leather bags and accessories. Across the street is the Murphy Arts Center, which comes alive on First Fridays. Nearby, the adorable Tuggle's Gifts & Goods has lots of Indiana-centric merchandise alongside fun gifts. Come back to the area in the evening to experience a different side of Fountain Square—its bustling restaurants, vintage duckpin bowling, and venues for live music.

Howl + Hide

1046 Virginia Ave., 463-224-9518
howlandhidesupply.com

Murphy Arts Center

1043 Virginia Ave., 317-638-2000
themurphyartscenter.com

Rooftop Fruit

1058 Virginia Ave.
rooftopfruit.co

Snakeroot Botanicals

1052 Virginia Ave., 317-604-7562
snakerootbotanicals.com

Square Cat Vinyl

1054 Virginia Ave., 317-875-1314
squarecatvinyl.com

Tuggle's Gifts & Goods

1029 Virginia Ave., 317-602-2820
tugglesgiftsandgoods.com

Zodiac Vintage

1060 Virginia Ave., 317-306-9600

START AN AFFORDABLE ART COLLECTION
AT TINY

Each December, the Indy Arts Council's Gallery 924 hosts TINY, an art show where every piece is smaller than six inches cubed. The size limitation enables the council to showcase about 500 pieces from more than 100 Indiana artists. But for customers, the wide selection is only part of the appeal. Because the pieces are small, they're also affordable—making it possible to start an art collection on a budget. Most pieces cost $100 or less. The artworks, including paintings, jewelry, and sculptures, also make perfect holiday gifts that are truly one of a kind. TINY is rightfully popular, so come early on opening day (the December First Friday) to snap up your favorite pieces before somebody else does.

924 N Pennsylvania St., 317-631-3301
indyarts.org/about/spaces/gallery-924

FIND A UNIQUE ANTIQUE AT MIDLAND

Ignore the decrepit exterior and poorly maintained parking lot. Inside the sprawling Midland Arts & Antiques Market, you'll find two (very creaky) floors of vendor booths selling antique furniture, lighting, and home decor. There's a large selection of vintage clothing and accessories, including jewelry and bags. The market also stocks glassware, artwork, books, toys, and collectible signage. Prices are reasonable, and booths sometimes have sales. Pro tip: Avoid hot days, when the second floor especially can be stifling despite the fans throughout the building.

907 E Michigan St., 317-267-9005

TIP

Follow the Midland Arts & Antiques Market on social media to get a peek at new items as they arrive.

SHOP BROAD RIPPLE

These days, the main drag in Broad Ripple is mostly bars. But if you stroll the tree-shaded back streets north of the strip, you'll discover perfectly flaky croissants at Rene's Bakery, flavored popcorn at Just Pop In, all-natural popsicles at Nicey Treat, and gourmet ice cream at BRICS (which is located in a former train depot along the Monon Trail). Vintage finds await at Broad Ripple Vintage and Satellite Vintage, while Rusted Moon Outfitters will equip you for your next hiking trip. Clothing boutiques like Lola Blu, 8Fifteen, Lark & Lily, and Marigold serve the fashionable crowd, while gift shops such as Artifacts and the Bungalow focus on artisan goods. When you work up an appetite, head to Petite Chou, a French bistro and champagne bar; Bazbeaux, a beloved pizza joint; or Broad Ripple Brewpub, which launched the local microbrewery scene. Another great option is the Cake Bake Shop, a restaurant fairyland with memorable desserts.

TIP

Broad Ripple Avenue has a few shopping holdouts, including the Pitaya clothing store, the Three Dog Bakery for pet treats, and the beloved Indy CD & Vinyl.

8Fifteen

815 E 65th St.
317-253-1234
8fifteen.com

Artifacts

6327 Guilford Ave.
317-255-1178
artifactsindy.com

BRICS (Broad Ripple Ice Cream Station)

901 E 64th St.
317-257-5757
bricsindy.com

Broad Ripple Vintage

824 E 64th St.
317-255-4135
broadripplevintage.com

The Bungalow

924 E Westfield Blvd.
317-253-5028
thebungalowinc.com

Just Pop In

6406 Cornell Ave.
317-257-9338
justpopinpopcorn.com

Lark & Lily Boutique

6358 Guilford Ave.
812-718-6574
larkandlilyboutique.com

Lola Blu Boutique

6350 Cornell Ave.
317-426-2116
lolabluboutique.com

Marigold

6512 Cornell Ave.
317-254-9939
marigoldclothing.com

Nicey Treat

833 E Westfield Blvd.
317-602-6423
niceytreat.com

Rene's Bakery

6524 Cornell Ave.
317-251-2253
facebook.com/renesbakery

Rusted Moon Outfitters

6410 Cornell Ave.
317-253-4453
rustedmoonindy.com

Satellite Vintage

824 E Westfield Blvd.
marketvintageindy.com

BUY BOOKS TO SUPPORT A WORTHY CAUSE
AT INDY READS

When Fountain Square lost its neighborhood library branch in 2020, Indy Reads stepped forward to fill the literary gap. The nonprofit organization created a vibrant storefront on Virginia Avenue stocking both new and used titles, making a special effort to highlight writers from marginalized communities. Purchases and donations support the organization's larger mission—community programs focused on literacy, job readiness, and English language skills. Check the busy calendar for events such as book club meetings, open mic nights, writing workshops, and author visits.

1066 Virginia Ave., 317-384-1496
indyreads.org

INDY'S INDIE BOOKSTORES

Golden Hour Books

A bright and airy bookshop in SoBro with insightful staff recommendations.

5208 N College Ave., 317-450-9894
goldenhourbooks.net

Kids Ink Children's Bookstore

A family favorite specializing in children's books, games, puzzles, and toys that encourage creative play.

5619 N Illinois St., 317-255-2598
kidsinkbooks.com

Loudmouth Books

A tiny safe haven for banned books, especially ones "for, by, and about marginalized people."

212 E 16th St., 317-492-9446
loudmouthindy.com

Pen & Pink Vintage

A Garfield Park bookshop specializing in vintage and antique books by women and Indiana authors.

2610 Shelby St., 317-416-0197
penandpinkvintage.square.site

Tomorrow Bookstore

A small but smartly curated Mass Ave gem with a section highlighting global authors.

882 Massachusetts Ave., 317-551-1893
bookshop.org/shop/tomorrowbookstore

SHOP DOWNTOWN ZIONSVILLE

With its quaint old buildings and historic brick Main Street, Zionsville might seem like a destination for antiques. Not so. The downtown district is home to shops selling modern clothing, jewelry, home decor, gifts, and much more. You'll find gourmet food items at Truffles & Creams, Grapevine Cottage, and Zionsville Olive Oil, while the cooperative Art IN Hand Gallery sells artwork by two dozen local artists. Crafters will enjoy Persnickety Stitchers and the Village Yarn Company, while literary types can browse Black Dog Books (for used and rare editions) and the Curious Squirrel Bookshop (for children and young adults). Abby's Garden Parties even stocks plants and other supplies for do-it-yourself terrariums. Along the way are many great restaurants and bakeries, including The Baker's House and My Sugar Pie.

Abby's Garden Parties
40 E Poplar St.
317-670-3623
abbysgardenparties.com

Art IN Hand Gallery
211 S Main St.
317-733-8426
artinhandgallery.com

The Baker's House
365 S Main St.
463-348-2299
bakershousebread.com

Black Dog Books
115 S Main St.
317-733-1747
blackdogbooksin.com

Curious Squirrel Bookshop
120 S Main St.
765-680-1051

Grapevine Cottage
61 S Main St.
317-733-1010
zionsville.grapevinecottage.com

My Sugar Pie
40 E Pine St.
317-733-8717
mysugarpie.com

Persnickety Stitchers
58A N Main St.
317-873-5010
persnicketystitchers.com

Truffles & Creams
55 E Pine St.
317-560-6355
trufflesandcreams.com

Village Yarn Company
209 S Main St.
317-873-0004
villageyarncompany.wordpress.com

Zionsville Olive Oil
31 E Pine St.
317-973-5583
zionsvilleoliveoil.com

SHOP CARMEL'S ARTS & DESIGN DISTRICT

Centered on the intersection of Main Street and Rangeline Road, the Carmel Arts & Design District is worth the trek north—if you can overlook the creepy human statues. Art galleries in the area include Art on Main Gallery & Gifts, the CCA Gallery, and the Magdalena Gallery of Art. Indiana Artisan, a statewide organization that recognizes the best of Hoosier craftsmanship, also has a gallery here. Peace Water Winery has a tasting room, Silver in the City stocks fun jewelry and gifts, and Xchocol'Art offers chocolate treats. Nearby, the Indiana Design Center is a complex of interior design showrooms that has become a regional destination. For dining along the way, try local favorites Bazbeaux Pizza or Bub's Burgers & Ice Cream.

Art on Main Gallery & Gifts
111 W Main St., 317-564-4115

Bazbeaux Pizza
111 W Main St., 317-848-4488
carmel.bazbeaux.com

Bub's Burgers & Ice Cream
210 W Main St., 317-706-2827
bubsburgers.com

CCA Gallery
111 W Main St., 317-844-2388
ccaartgallery.com

Indiana Artisan
22 N Rangeline Rd., 317-964-9455
indianaartisan.org

Indiana Design Center
200 S Rangeline Rd., 317-569-5975
indianadesigncenter.com

Magdalena Gallery of Art
27 E Main St., 317-844-0005
magdalenagallery.com

Peace Water Winery
37 W Main St., 317-810-1330
peacewaterwinery.com

Silver in the City
111 W Main St., 317-993-3669
silverinthecity.com

Xchocol'Art
211 First St. SW, 317-443-3029
xchocolart.com

100

SHOP CARMEL'S CITY CENTER

Anchored by the Center for the Performing Arts, Carmel's City Center development is a compact cluster of shops and restaurants that makes for an easy stroll. Housewares purveyor Addendum has two shopfronts here, one specializing in checkered MacKenzie-Childs pottery. Meanwhile, Out of the Blue stocks beautiful hand-painted pottery imported from Poland. Kits & Kaboodle sells toys, and the Linden Tree stocks gifts and housewares. Hey Little Diddle also has two shopfronts, one selling clothes for babies and the other clothes for older children. Several other shops stock clothing and jewelry. When you need a break, restaurant options include the whimsical Cake Bake Shop and the ever-popular Divvy.

Addendum

800 S Rangeline Rd. and 751 Hanover Place
317-253-3400

The Cake Bake Shop

799 Hanover Place, 317-257-2253
thecakebakeshop.com

Divvy

71 City Center Dr., 317-706-0000
divvycarmel.com

Hey Little Diddle Baby

736 Hanover Place, 317-564-4858
heylittlediddle.com

Hey Little Diddle Child

730 S Rangeline Rd., 317-564-0083
heylittlediddle.com

Kits & Kaboodle

723 Hanover Place, 317-566-8101
kitsandkaboodletoys.com

Linden Tree

736 Hanover Place, 317-773-3238
lindentreegifts.com

Out of the Blue Polish Pottery

719 Hanover Place, 317-853-6349
outofthebluepottery.com

A buffalo fountain on Monument Circle
Courtesy of Kelly Harris, Indiana Landmarks

SUGGESTED ITINERARIES

ACTIVE ADVENTURES

ARTSY EXPERIENCES

DATE NIGHTS

ESSENTIAL INDIANAPOLIS

FAMILY FUN

HISTORY LESSONS

ACTIVITIES BY SEASON

SPRING

SUMMER

FALL

WINTER

INDEX